HOW TO HAVE A POOL BUILT

STEP BY STEP HOW IT IS DONE

By: STAN BLAKENEY

Copyright: July 31, 2017

Revision 15

PREFACE

This is the process of planning and building a swimming pool. It will take you all the way from having just an idea about owning a pool, through planning, financing, construction and getting back to normal afterward. I will tell you of the problems I encountered along the way and what I did afterward to enhance my pool. If nothing else, I hope you enjoy just seeing what all is involved in building a swimming pool.

July 31, 2017

TABLE OF CONTENTS

1. PLANNING THE POOL

The first thing to consider is, can you afford a pool? If you are paying cash, then you might want to consider if your money might well be spent somewhere else. Like adding an addition to the house or maybe paying for your children's college. If you are going to be financing, are you going to put any money down? If not, how much a month can you afford to pay? What about interest rates? Can you get a loan with an interest rate you can live with?

Another thing to consider is the added value to your home. What, if any, will a pool add to the value of your home? Believe it or not, most of the time the extra value added to your home is negligible. Some people will not by a home with a pool, while others think of it as a great asset to the house. I guess they envision themselves setting out by the pool with the kids swimming in the summertime.

Now let's consider where you live. If you live up north, you will have to consider if it will be worth having a pool. First of all, the summertime where the weather is warm enough to enjoy swimming is a lot shorter up north than say in Texas, where you can swim from May through September. Sure, you can have a heated pool, but can you afford the extra cost to heat a pool? These are all things you must consider before having a pool put in.

If you go ahead and decide on having a pool built, you must now consider what kind of destruction will be caused by the construction of your pool.

In my case, I had a sprinkler system that was destroyed in four different places in my yard. You and your builder must decide on who is going to pay for repairs and who is going to do the repairs if you have any damage in your yard. I decided to do the repairs myself since I am the one who originally installed my sprinkler system. I wanted the repairs done correctly. Digging up your yard to fix a faulty repair is not my idea of having fun.

The next thing is deciding on a pool company to do the work. This is entirely up to you. The one consideration I gave to my company was; is this a national company? Are they backed by a large corporation nationwide? What kind of reputation do they have, both locally and nationally? Check out their references. See if other local customers are satisfied with not only the construction but every aspect of the process. Finally, when you do decide on a builder, NEVER pay upfront. Most lenders will issue checks for the different steps of the construction. In other words, once the step is completed, the lender will give you a check. This is for your protection.

Now that you have a pool company selected, call and make an appointment. The person who comes to your house should be knowledgeable about the design and construction of your pool. They should also be able to help you with any unusual aspects of the build, like a sprinkler system, fences, access, etc. He or she will also take all your information for financing at this time unless you plan on making arrangements to have it financed yourself.

Once you have settled on a final design, your plans will be turned over to a structural engineer and blueprints will be drawn up. Any changes will usually be made before this time.

We were next sent to a lawyer who handled all the loan papers. Why a lawyer you ask? Well, the loan company puts a lien on your home until the loan is paid off. The reason for this is it is hard to repossess a swimming pool. We signed all the papers and were now ready to start the process.

2. GETTING READY FOR CONSTRUCTION

I put up a new eight-foot-high fence straight across the back and down the right side of the yard. I also did the right front gate. Now when they finish, all I have to do is build the left side and across the left front where all the equipment entered and exited the back yard during the build.

I took down the front fence and the post in the center on the left side after we signed all the paperwork.

When I put my sprinkler system in, I left room for a pool in the right end of the back yard. That way there would only be minor sprinkler line moving when the time came. After he showed me where the pool would extend to, I realized I was going to have to move a couple of sprinkler lines. The pool was going to be a little larger than what I planned for when I put in my sprinkler system.

My pool was going to be 23 feet wide at the shallow end and 12 feet wide at the deep end. It will be 33 feet long and hold around 25,000 gallons of water.

Moving the sprinkler lines in preparation for the pool

Moving sprinkler lines

Another view across the back yard

A view toward the shed

Another view looking to the east

The next step was for the gas company, electric company and the telephone company to come out and mark all their underground lines. This was to keep the pool company from cutting the utility lines.

The utilities have been marked

Fence removed and utilities marked

Next, the pool company is going to come out and layout the pool in orange spray paint so the excavators will know how to dig the pool.

The pool is laid out in orange paint

The pool is laid out in orange spray paint

Now comes the construction equipment. They used a track hoe and two Bob Cats. The first thing they did after unloading the equipment was to dig up the shrubbery across the front where the fence was. They put down 2X4s on each side of the sidewalk to keep the track hoe from breaking the sidewalk. That did not help my sprinkler lines. I had to repair the line running horizontally to the street that the track hoe broke.

When they dug up the shrubs they cut my pressurized one-inch line plus a ¾ inch line and the wiring to the controller. Oh well, just something else to fix.

One of the dump trucks with the two Bob Cats

The second dump truck with the track hoe

3. EXCAVATION BEGINS

The track hoe digging out the shrubs

Now they are going to grade off the land and dig out where the patio around the pool will go. This also destroyed two pressurized one-inch sprinkler lines. I repaired them that night. It was October by now and sunlight was gone by about 6:00 p.m.

Grading the yard in prep for setting up pool outline

More prepping the yard for digging the pool

They are now starting to set up the outline of the pool

**They are almost through completing the border
of the pool**

Now that they had the outline of the pool set up and leveled, it was time to start digging the pool. They started with the deep end which was farthest away from them. They would then work their way to the shallow end.

When They started the deep end, they hit three gigantic rocks about three feet down. One on the left side, one on the right side, and one at the end. It was almost dark by now and I could tell that they were a little tired and grumpy. The head guy said they would bring a Jack Hammer attachment back tomorrow to break up those big rocks. He said, "It costs $200.00 an hour to use the Jack Hammer attachment." I spent the rest of the night wondering how much that was going to cost me.

Well, they showed up about 10:30 a.m. the next morning and seemed to be in a lot better mood. The guy in charge said he was going to try to hit those rocks with the bucket on the track hoe and break them off. If that worked I would not have to pay for the Jack Hammer. Thank God it worked. Boy was I relieved.

**Breaking off the three rocks and digging
the deep end**

The big rocks gone, he can now continue digging

He is almost finished with the deep end

**Dumping dirt behind him so the Bob Cat
can scoop it up**

Just about finished with the dig

Deep end complete, starting to take shape

Shallow end complete

They have finished but there is still a lot of mess

Here you can see the complete pool

The next step is to install the plumbing and the steel, called rebar. The pipes stick out of the pool about a foot and are capped. This is so they can pressure test the pipes to ensure there are no leaks. The skimmer is installed, the main drain, the concrete slab, and the pump and filter are also installed. The rebar is put into the pool to add strength to the gunite (concrete).

4. REBAR AND PLUMBING IS INSTALLED

The plumbing and rebar (steel) is installed

Another view of the rebar and plumbing

**They used pieces of brick to hold the rebar
up off the ground**

The pump and filter installed

They next came out and installed a ground wire which hooked up to the rebar and then ran underground to the back of the pump motor which will be grounded. The next step will be to gunite the pool.

5. GUNITE IS SPRAYED

The gunite pump truck

Gunite being pumped to the back yard

Starting to gunite the pool

Spraying gunite

More spraying gunite

They are about halfway through with the gunite

About three-fourths done

Finishing up the gunite

The pool is covered to help cure the gunite

Another picture – notice the new 8-foot-high fence

The gunite is now cured enough that work can continue. Notice the four holes that you can see at the bottom of the pool. There are two more further down in the deep end. These allow water to seep into the pool until they plaster the pool. The reason for this is to keep the pool from floating like a boat and rising up out of the ground. Notice the water already in the deep end.

The gunite is finished

Here you can see the water in the deep end

Next comes the coping and tile. The tile and coping would be selected when you are planning the pool. If you want decorative tiles on your steps and love seats, go purchase the designs you want at a local tile store. Be sure to purchase enough to do the job. It is better to have a few leftovers than to not have enough.

Have your decorative patterns laid out on the steps and love seats before the tile guy shows up. Now use your bargaining skills to work out a deal with the tile guy to have yours installed. It cost me $50.00 and I used some of my left-over tiles. Had I known what I am telling you, I would have gone to a tile store and picked out some decorative tile. It took him two days to do the job.

6. COPING AND TILE IS INSTALLED

Here the coping and tile has been installed

The shallow end of the pool with coping and tile installed – notice the Love seat on the left and the steps on the right with another Love seat

Another view – notice the steps and love seat

7. ELECTRICAL IS INSTALLED

Now comes the electrical. They ran conduit from the breaker box to the control box by the pump and filter. They also ran wires through the attic and down underground to the pool light. I had a fiber optics light installed. I wish I had not done that. It is not anywhere near as bright as a regular pool light. With a regular bulb, you have to drain the pool down enough to get to the light fixture in order to change the bulb. With the fiber optics light, everything is in a box above ground. While the electricians were wiring everything, I had them install a two-plug receptacle on each side of the house. That came in handy later on. If you need extra receptacles or outside lights installed for your pool area, this would be a good time to work a deal with your electricians. They are already there and usually, the work done will be a lot cheaper.

The fiber optics box for the pool light

Another picture of the fiber optics light

Here the electrical is installed

8. POOL DECK IS PREPARED FOR CONCRETE

Next comes the pool deck. Now is the time to talk to the guy who is going to install or pour your deck. If you want more deck than is in the contract, work a side deal with the contractor. I was having brushed concrete poured. I negotiated a deal to have about 200 square feet more concrete poured. It is usually not much more than the cost of the extra concrete. This is the time to do it.

**The contractor has brought in sand
for the cushion base**

Another view of the sand

The deck is laid out for paving

The deck is ready to pour

Another view of the deck ready to pour

Deck ready to pour

9. CONCRETE IS POURED

Concrete has just been poured

Concrete has set up

They then sent a crew out to clean up the pool and the yard. They raked the yard of all the left-over rocks and cleaned out all the trash that had ended up in the pool during construction.

10. POOL AND YARD ARE CLEANED UP

The pool and yard are cleaned up

The pool ready for plaster

Plastering is next in the process. They showed up that morning and plastered the pool. They immediately started filling the pool with water when they finished.

11. POOL IS PLASTERED

A crew is plastering the pool

They are still plastering

Just about finished

12. FILLING AND BRUSHING THE POOL

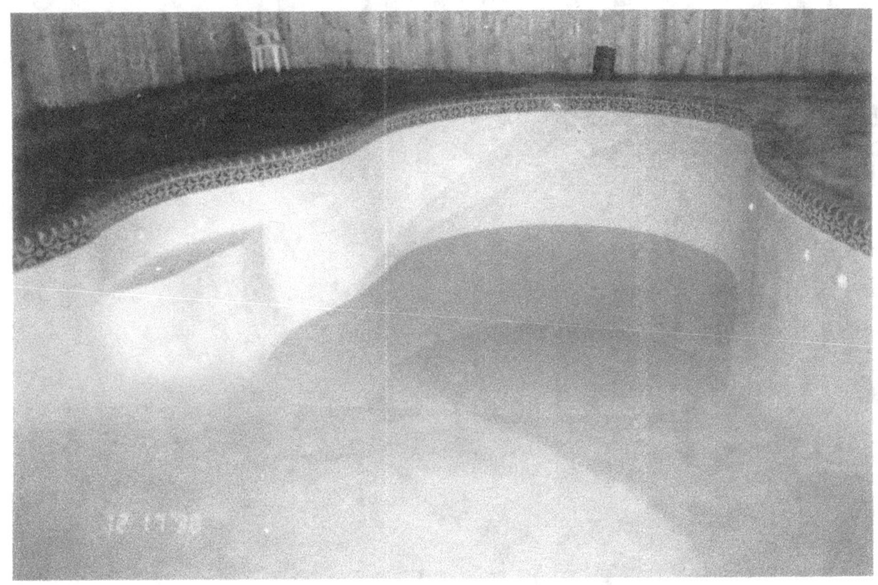

Finished and started filling with water

Water is slowly rising

A view of the steps with the tile placed in the plaster

The pool is filled

The pool people came out and put a whole bunch of muriatic acid in the pool. They also left me a brush and said to brush the pool completely every day for a week. The reason was to remove loose plaster from the pool. It was January when they finished the pool and it was cold as heck. I thought I was going to freeze to death before that week was up.

The pool finished

Another view of the pool

The shallow end of the pool

Pool furniture provided by the pool company

13. FINISHING THE FENCE

I started building the fence again after finishing the pool.

The fence is almost done

Another view of the pool

A better view of how far along the fence is

The fence is now complete

14. POOL FINISHED

Pool finished

Notice sprinkler valve box sticking up

Another view of the pool

Another view

Side yard cleaned up and new dirt spread

Pool finished

15. FLOWER BED BUILD

Flower bed being built

Another view of the flower bed

Flower bed down the back of the pool

16. BUILDING THE PATIO

Dirt now filled in around sprinkler box

Working on wall and patio

Patio and wall nearing completion

More of patio build

More of the patio build

Another view

The patio is getting closer to completion

Patio almost finished

17. PATIO FINISHED

Patio is finished

Pool finished, grass growing

Another view

Pool and patios finished

THE END

ABOUT THE AUTHOR

Stan Blakeney dedicated almost 14 years of his life to Braniff International Airlines before becoming a Civil Service WG-13 Avionics technician and Air Force Reserves Master Sergeant. He retired after 35 years of Military Service and 30 years of Civil Service. Originally from Jackson, Mississippi, he has lived in the Fort Worth, Texas area since 1976. He has been married to his wife Nila since 1991. They have three grown children, five grandchildren and three great-grandchildren. They also have several pampered kitty cats.

OTHER BOOKS BY STAN BLAKENEY

Search Stan Blakeney at Amazon.com for a complete list of formats and titles.

MY LIFE AS I REMEMBER IT

December 31, 2016

This book is a brief story of the highlights of my life from infancy in Mississippi to retiring from the U.S. Government and the Air Force Reserves. If I included everything I can think of that happened from infancy to now, this book would be a thousand pages long. So, it includes most of the things that I considered important or maybe interesting. I specifically wanted to include courses I have taken while both active duty and in the Reserves. I also wanted to include the places I have lived, the vehicles I have owned and the jobs I have had.

I have lost a handful of close friends in the last few years and it really opens your eyes as to just how short life is. I wanted to get all this down on paper, not only for my family and friends but believe it or not, for myself.

If you read this book, you probably already know me. So, I hope you learn something about me you did not know and enjoy reading about things that happened in my life.

THE ABDUCTION OF JOHN CONWAY

July 12, 2018

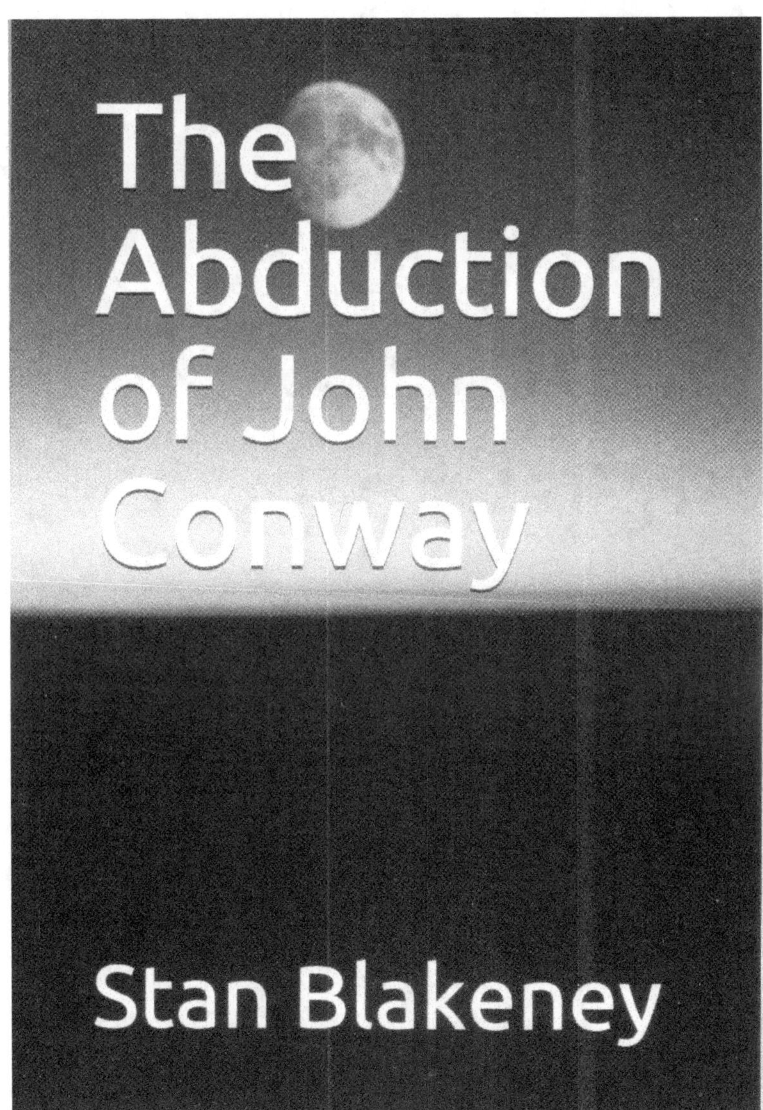

John was a typical husband living the American dream. He had a good job, a wife, two beautiful daughters whom he dearly loved and a nice home in North Dallas.

Then, without warning, his life was turned upside down. He could not believe what was happening to him. From finding out he had pancreatic cancer, to being abducted by aliens and taken to a galaxy far, far away. Then to top it off, he was put on display like an animal. What else could they do to him? Will John ever make it home, or will he be doomed to a life on another planet? Find out.

MIKE DAWSON – INVISIBLE MAN

August 19, 2018

Mike Dawson is your average bachelor. He has a degree in Electrical Engineering, a great job, and lives in Tucson, Arizona. He has a girlfriend named Shirley that he has been with about five years.

His life is turned upside down when a meteor crashes onto his property while he and Shirley watch.

He started robbing drug dealers and banks to get a lot of money. Find out what he does with the money?

He is eventually caught with counterfeit money by the Secret Service and is arrested. Can Mike get out of this predicament? Find out.

BE CAREFUL WHAT YOU WISH FOR

February 20, 2019

Suppose you had a chance to become one of the Beatles today. Would you take it? These guys did. See how they handled fame and how it affected their lives and friendships. Can they maintain their sanity with the same stress and success that destroyed the Beatles? What will they do to return things to normal without breaking up the group? Find out.

OUR FRIEND FROM ANOTHER WORLD

AUGUST 14, 2019

Our Friend
From
Another
World

Stan Blakeney

Bill and Betty Johnson were hard-working farmers in 1880 West Texas. They had four children, two boys and two girls. Then one day their life was changed forever. They met a creature from outer space. The only thing different about him was his looks. He was kind-hearted, very smart and could do extraordinary things with some of the items he had with him. He was stranded here on Earth and needed help getting home. The Johnsons were his only hope. Find out if they can get him home.

HOW TO CLEAN AND SERVICE YOUR HAYWARD D.E. POOL FILTER

April 24, 2020

This book will show you how to completely disassemble, clean, inspect, reassemble and service your Hayward D.E. series filter. All of the Hayward D.E. series filters are basically the same thing. The differences are the length of the *Upper Filter Bodies*, the *Retainment Rods*, the *Filter Elements* and the *Outlet Elbows*. The **D.E. 2420** uses 12″ filters, the **D.E. 3620** uses 18″ filters, the **D.E. 4820** uses 24″ filters, the **D.E. 6020** uses 30″ filters and the **D.E. 7220** uses 36″ filters. In these instructions, I will use my Hayward **D.E. 6020** filter. With proper care and cleaning, your Hayward filter should give you many years of reliable service.

UNUSUAL STORIES OF AN AIRCRAFT AVIONICS TECHNICIAN

April 3, 2022

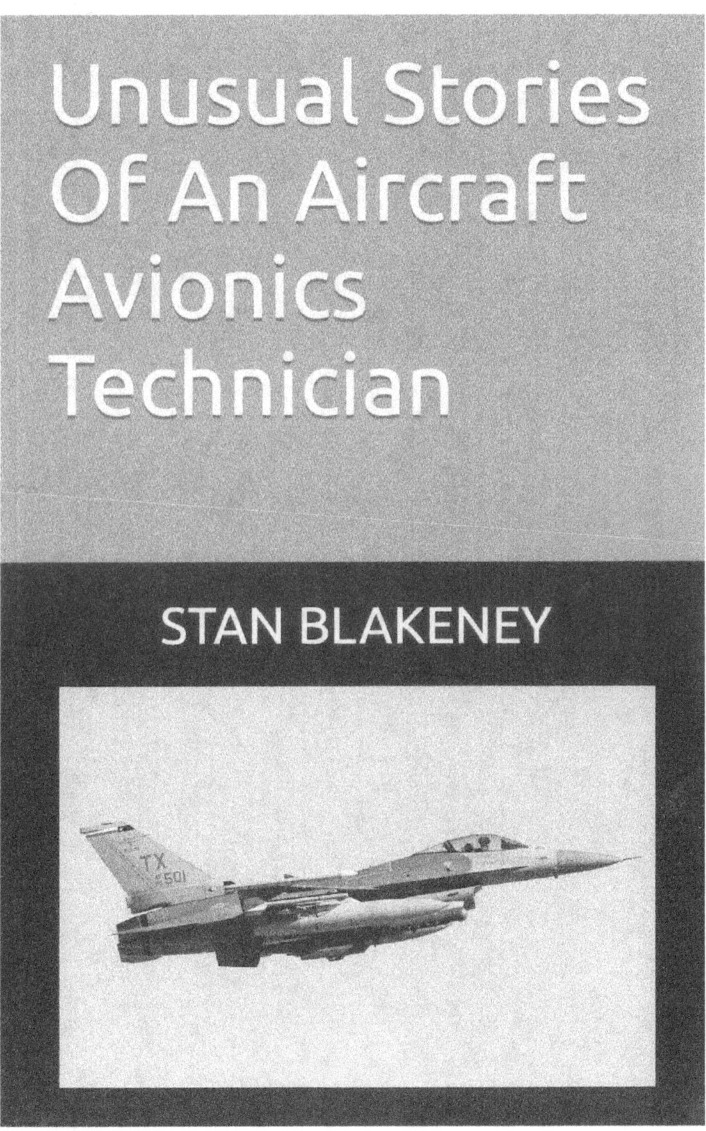

This book will show you how unusual problems are troubleshot. I will try to explain how the system works and how we are going about the process of finding the problem. I tried to make it as simple and interesting as possible. If you have a mechanical or electrical ability, you should be able to follow along with no problem. If you are an aircraft mechanic, you should have little difficulty keeping up with me. If you are thinking of becoming an Avionics Technician, this book will give you an idea of some of the problems you may encounter in your job. Hope you enjoy.

MY TIME WITH BRANIFF INTERNATIONAL AIRLINES

June 22, 2024

This book starts out with a brief history of Braniff International Airlines. It then shows you most of the equipment that is being used on the ground at all the major airports around the world.

From there I will let you visualize what the life of a 727-100 at DFW (Dallas/Fort Worth) airport was like in 1982 during the 25-minute turn around. From the time it rolls into the gate and is chocked, until the chocks are pulled and it is pushed out of the gate.

Then, I will share all of the ordinary or maybe even funny stories that happened to me in my almost 14 years at Braniff and what I did for a living after Braniff's demise.